M000217050

Church Growth Made Simple

Twenty
Simple Changes
Guaranteed to
Transform
Your Church

by
George O. McCalep, Jr., Ph.D.

Orman Press
Lithonia, Georgia

Church Growth Made Simple
Twenty Simple Changes Guaranteed to Transform Your Church
by
George O. McCalep, Jr., Ph.D.

Copyright © 2005
Orman Press, Inc.

ISBN: 1-891773-67-4

Scripture quotations are taken from THE HOLY BIBLE, *King James Version*. Bible quotations marked NIV are from the Holy Bible, New International Version, copyright © 1973, 1978, 1984 Zondervan Publishing House.

All rights reserved. No part of this publication may be reproduced, stored in a retrieval system, or transmitted in any form or by any means, electronic, mechanical, photo-copying, recording, or otherwise, without the prior written permission of the copyright owner.

Printed in the United States of America

10 9 8 7 6 5 4 3 2 1

Orman Press, Inc.
Lithonia, Georgia

Table of Contents

Introduction 3

Change 1 13
    Change the Worship Music From Art to Heart

Change 2 17
    Change to a Boardless Governance

Change 3 21
    Change the Selection Process for Church Leaders
    to a Gift-Based Ministry

Change 4 27
    Change from Teacher-Oriented to Growth and
    Purpose-Oriented Bible Study

Change 5 31
    Change to Embrace the Creative Arts

Change 6 37
    Change to Embrace Technology

Change 7 43
    Change to a Coaching Empowerment
    Leadership Style

Change 8 49
    Change from Being Maintenance-Driven
    to Ministry-Driven

Change 9 55
    Change to Embrace Missions as a Lifestyle

Change 10 59
    Change the Worship Style to Expressive
    and Participatory

Table of Contents

Change 11 65
Change Something for the Sake of Change

Change 12 71
Change to a Systematic Strategy to Grow in Giving

Change 13 75
Change to a Social Conscience and
the Gospel of Liberation

Change 14 81
Change from Being Membership-Oriented to
Discipleship-Oriented

Change 15 85
Change to Embrace the Holy Spirit and
Acknowledge Spiritual Warfare

Change 16 91
Change to Intentionally Prioritize Relationships

Change 17 97
Change from Secular Order and Authority to
Divine Order and Spiritual Authority

Change 18 105
Change from Casual Isolated Planning to
Strategic Team Planning

Change 19 111
Change Biased Perceptions of Church Growth

Change 20 119
Change to a Marketing Orientation and
Intentional Evangelism

Notes 124

Church Growth Made Simple

Twenty Simple Changes Guaranteed to Transform Your Church

The key to church growth is change. Our icon illustrates
a sign language symbol for change. It is a motion that
inverts one's hands from one position to a similar, but
opposite position. This motion conveys that change is
constant, not static. Any church that wants to grow must
be willing to constantly change.

INTRODUCTION

"Church growth means all that is involved in bringing men and women who do not have a personal relationship with Jesus Christ into fellowship with Him and into responsible church membership."[1]

C. PETER WAGNER

Have you ever wondered why some churches are growing, and others are standing still and even declining? The primary reason is their inability to change. Some pastors and congregations are unwilling to change, while others simply don't know what or how to change.

Many books have been written concerning the need for change and the dynamics of change. However, this book is for those who want to change and grow, but don't know what to change. Church Growth Made Simple offers twenty simple changes that can result in immediate growth when implemented in a willing environment. All twenty changes cannot be implemented simultaneously. Therefore, a flexible implementation should be established. Additionally, the church and leadership should develop an opportunistic posture relative to change.

> Church growth can be simple. However, you must be able to change, and change is not easy.

These twenty changes are designed to ignite any church, especially one stagnated in traditionalism. Although all twenty of the changes may not be feasible for your church, an attempt should be made to implement all of them to some degree. In doing so, enough fire will be ignited between one and twenty for you to detect a new and refreshing pattern of growth.

There is no magic in church growth. Church growth can be simple. However, you must be able to change, and change is not easy. Church growth has only one price tag. It is called "change." This book is based on the premise that growth cannot take place without change. Be well assured that growth will not occur without change. This reality must be internalized before these twenty changes can be implemented.

Also, the church is a living organism, and organisms grow. If organisms don't grow and reproduce, they become extinct and die. This necessary change is not a one-time occurrence. Rather, it is continuously necessary for growth to continuously occur.

> When a church hits a plateau, it will soon begin to decline, which means it is time to look for possible changes.

The question each pastor and congregation must ask is: Is our church growing? The answer is determined by examining the trend in your financial contributions over past years. Financial contributions have proven to be a reliable measurement for church growth. If there is not at least a five percent increase in actual giving each year, growth is not occurring, and change is the only solution. Many churches make the mistake of believing that they can simply do what they are doing better. A classic definition of stupidity is doing the same thing over and over again, yet expecting different results. If you tried it and it did not work, then change it.

Plateaus

Churches are subject to plateaus. A church reaches a plateau when its growth has leveled. When a church hits a plateau, it will soon begin to decline, which means it is time to look for possible changes. The church that I have been blessed to pastor for the last twenty-five years hit several plateaus in her growth from twenty-five members to over six thousand members. First, there was the 100-member plateau, then the 500-member plateau, and the 1,000-member plateau. I believe plateaus that occur between 800–1,200 members are the most difficult to overcome because they often mean a change in facility and possibly location.

After we broke through the 1,000-member plateau, we did not hit another plateau until we reached 2,500 hundred members. Then, there was the 4,000-member plateau and finally the 6,000-

> **Change always takes place at the spiritual level; never at the natural level of flesh.**

member plateau. At each plateau, change was required to move forward. Currently, plans are being made for a change in facility to move us to what I anticipate to be a difficult breakthrough.

The question is: Has your church reached a plateau? If you have or if you anticipate reaching a plateau in the near future, this book will be of great help to you.

Change: Natural vs. Supernatural

Change is a curse word in many churches. The natural man cannot change because it is natural for the flesh to resist change. Only the spiritual man can change. Change always takes place at the spiritual level; never at the natural level of flesh. A congregation that is not spiritually prepared for change will be unable to successfully implement these twenty changes. According to Elmer Towns, John Maxwell often states that people change when they (1) hurt enough that they have to change; (2) learn enough that they want to change; and (3) receive enough that they are able to change.[2] The following describes three cardinal rules that should be followed when preparing for change.

> **The believer doesn't change based on human direction, but will change in obedience to the Word of God.**

Cardinal Rule #1:

Don't change anything until you teach the biblical principle that supports the change.

Believers change if they learn that the Bible teaches or explains a particular change. For example, simply getting believers who grew up in a traditional Calvinistic church to give God a "hand clap of praise" could be challenging because the clapping of hands was considered applauding man, not God, in their former Christian experience, and was therefore prohibited. It may have even been considered an activity of the anti-Christ. However, when believers learn in Psalm 47:1 that giving God a hand clap of praise is a weapon in spiritual warfare, their minds are transformed.

The believer doesn't change based on human direction, but will change in obedience to the Word of God. Again, the absolute cardinal rule is: Don't try to change anything unless the change is justified by Scripture. The flip side of this coin is that non-believers will not change based on scriptural justification because they don't believe the Bible in the first place. Those of us who are instruments of change in our churches must realize that non-believers (unsaved people who have never been spiritually converted, or experienced the power of regeneration or born again), cannot and will not change until they experience the change necessary to become true believers. Therefore, a word of wisdom to those who are instruments of change in your churches: Don't waste your time dealing with change. Concentrate on making believers. People cannot become disciples until they are first believers.

> **Repentance always precedes transformation.**

Cardinal Rule #2:

Repentance always precedes transformation.

The next step in spiritually preparing to change is repentance. Repentance always precedes transformation. Many Christians feel that because they are saved they are beyond repentance. They understand repentance to be necessary for salvation. They feel that because they repented when they were saved, it is not necessary to repent again. Repentance was necessary for the transformation that occurred at the time of salvation and is necessary for any other improvement or deliverances that take place in our Christian journey. We only need to be saved once, but we need multiple deliverances. Therefore, repentance must be reoccurring.

Each time we go to church or enter into God's presence, we should leave a better person because some degree of transformation has taken place. Most of us go to church and leave with no spiritual change. We may receive some inspiration and information, but if there is no repentance there will be no transformation. As pastor of the Greenforest Community Baptist Church for the past twenty-five years, I have to repent many times for wrong thinking in my pastoral leadership as well as repenting daily as an individual. I was wrong about the relationship of expressive praise to biblical worship. I was wrong relative to my ignorance concerning spiritual gifts. I was wrong about neglecting my family in my passion to serve the church. I was wrong about the inflexibility of pastors to change. As a matter of fact, part of the inspiration for this book grew out of my wrong thinking about pastors' unwillingness to change. God revealed to me that there are many pastors—young and old—who are more than willing to change if they only knew what to change and how to change it.

Cardinal Rule #3:

Prayer must undergird the entire change process.

A church that enters into a time of transformation without a strong undergirding of prayer is headed for a collision. We know there is power in prayer. The familiar saying is true: No prayer, no power. Little prayer, little power. Much prayer, much power. Prayer is essential to the change process. Every change that is to be implemented must first be undergirded (lifted up) and covered with prayer. The whole congregation should be asked to pray, and some prayer warriors should be designated to pray at specific times for specific things. Remember, not only is prayer essential to the success of the change process, but you cannot get too much of it. You don't have to worry about over praying.

> A Church that enters into a time of transformation without a strong undergirding of prayer is headed for a collision.

Summary

Change is difficult, yet it is a powerful and necessary essential in growing your church. In the spirit of God, I encourage you to begin implementing these twenty changes in obedience to God's command to grow. Pray to discern God's will for your church. Use pages 124–129 to record the changes He is directing you to make. Then, watch your church boldly overcome the plateau stronghold.

Discussion Questions

1. Is your church growing? What trends have you seen in financial contributions over the last three years?

2. Has your church reached a plateau? Are you in a decline? Why?

3. What is your church's attitude toward change?

4. Why must change occur on the spiritual level? Why does change not occur on the natural level of the flesh?

5. Why is it necessary to teach the biblical principle that supports a change before implementing that change?

6. Repentance always precedes transformation. Of what does your church need to repent?

7. If you want your church to grow, it begins with prayer. Discuss how you can assemble a team of prayer warriors and implement an intentional prayer strategy to bring about change in your church.

CHANGE 1

Change the Worship Music
from Art to Heart

first heard the term "music of the heart versus art" from Pastor Rick Warren when we both participated in a church growth conference in Dallas, Texas. Rick said that churches must bite the bullet relative to the predominant music of the church. He proclaimed "music of the heart" to be the predominant music of the black church and "music of the art" to be the predominant music of the white church. He went on to say that as the pastor of a predominantly white church, he had chosen heart over art. Although he initially lost some members, his gain tremendously out-weighed his losses.

> **Music of the heart is soulful music that sings directly to God rather than about God.**

Personally, I don't believe that the dichotomy of worship and church music is as absolute as my friend, Pastor Warren, asserts. However, he conveys a point that is worthy of discussion and should be applied to some degree. As the pastor of a fast-growing, predominantly black church, I have always insisted on a variety of music from our various choirs. However, the predominant style is definitely of the heart.

Music of the heart is not limited to any race of people. Music of the heart is soulful music that sings directly *to* God rather than *about* God. The lyrics of anthems and hymns are usually about God, rather than to God. Heart music, commonly referred to as praise music, is directed to God. Heart music gives love and adoration to God. Biblically and theologically speaking, loving God is the predominant command. Shouldn't music directing love to God be the predominant music of the church? There is value in all church music, but churches that want to grow spiritually and numerically should make music of the heart the primary music of the congregation.

Discussion Questions

1. What is the difference between music of the art and music of the heart?

2. Is it really necessary to change to music of the heart if it is not natural to your culture?

3. How can music of the heart help a church to grow?

4. What kind of worship music is predominantly sung in your church? If it is music of the art, what would it take to change to music of the heart? What difference would singing music of the heart make in your worship service?

CHANGE 2

Change to a Boardless Governance

This suggestion to become boardless is a dangerous, traumatic and dramatic change to implement, yet it might be the change that is most needed to transform any church from being stagnant to dynamic. Of all my twenty suggested changes, the cardinal rule of "don't change it until you teach the biblical principle that supports the change" applies most here.

Most churches are governed by boards. The problem is that boards operate from law, and God operates from love. Boards operate according to the letter of the law, and the church should operate according to the nature and spirit of Christ. People who serve on boards may be believers with good intentions, yet when faced with board responsibilities, they often lean on their own understanding of what is right. Also, boards tend to bring out the worst of our egos and desires to rule. It has been said that boards "board up the church."

> The problem is that boards operate from law, and God operates from love.

The church is an organism, not an organization. The church must be organized, but cannot be an organization. Organizations are bureaucratic. Organisms are spontaneous. For the church to grow, it needs the freedom and flexibility of spontaneity. There is no need to have board meetings to vote on things that Christ has already commanded us to do. Scripture does not mention a board or a chairman of the board. In addition, the word *trustee* is not a biblical term or position. Therefore, the idea of a boardless chair is to bring the governance of the church in compliance with Scripture.

When transforming to a boardless form of governance, believers typically ask, "Well, who is going to run the church?" The answer is: The servant-leaders led by the Holy Spirit and the Spirit-filled, God-fearing pastor, who is the chief servant. The issue should not be about control, but servant leadership. Church members may also ask, "Well what about the fiscal affairs of the church?" Most of the financial decisions usually made in board meetings can be resolved by a good budget that is planned and ratified with congregational participation.

Some churches think they must have a board to be incorporated based on federal and state law. This is not the case. To be incorporated, the Secretary of State simply requires the signature of three or more designated persons who would be responsible for legal matters. Legal matters have nothing to do with making day-to-day financial decisions and managing daily operations. Churches that want to grow would do well to implement a boardless form of government.

Discussion Questions

1. What problems do you see in the church because of having boards of governance?

2. How can your church organize under a boardless governance?

3. How could eliminating boards help your church to grow?

4. How would legal and financial decisions be handled in your church if it were under a boardless governance?

CHANGE 3

Change the Selection Process for Church Leaders to a Gift-based Ministry

How do you determine who is going to serve as a leader? Many churches have a nomination process where members are elected by a vote of the congregation. On the other end of the spectrum, the leaders of the church are appointed by the pastor . The fallacy of these methods is that they exclude the work of the Holy Spirit that gives spiritual gifts to believers for the work of the church. Therefore, a spiritual gifts ministry should be established and infused into any process that is used to select leaders.

The process of voting on people in the church should definitely be eliminated. In my book, *Faithful Over a Few Things: Seven Critical Church Growth Principles,* I explained the problem of voting on people in the church as follows:

> In most cases, voting on people for offices, positions, or any other reason results in one winner and many losers. There should be no losers in God's family. Voting on people will always damage relationships. Voting on issues can also damage relationships, if they are not spiritually discerned. The only vote on a person should come when the church votes to discern the will of God in the calling of a pastor. Afterwards, other methods and procedures should be established to select leadership positions. I fully realize that this may represent a radical change for some churches and denominations, but change is necessary for church growth. If voting on people damages

relationships, stifles growth, promotes competition and establishes a playing field for Satan, it should be eliminated in the church.[3]

The church is not and was never intended to be a democracy. Rather, the church is a theocracy, meaning it is "God-led." In the chapter on "Spiritual Authority," I will discuss further the need for the pastor (the God chosen leader of the church) to be given the necessary authority in the selection of leaders. The amount of authority exercised in the process will vary depending on the size of the church and the leadership style of the pastor. But again, the authority must be granted.

> The church is not and was never intended to be a democracy. Rather, the church is a theocracy, meaning it is "God-led."

Regardless of the authority given and exercised, the pastor and the process must consider spiritual gifts. Therefore, the pastor and/or whoever is selecting leaders must know the passion and spiritual gifts of those whom they are placing in leadership positions.

What are spiritual gifts, and what is a gift-based ministry? Spiritual gifts are God-given abilities for ministering effectively and pleasurably to others.[4] Effective ministering must be determined by other believers; pleasurably ministering can be self-determined. The Bible teaches that all believers are blessed with at least one spiritual gift.

> *But unto every one of us is given grace*
> *according to the measure of the gift of*
> *Christ. Wherefore he saith, When he*
> *ascended up on high, he led captivity*
> *captive, and gave gifts unto men*
> *(Ephesians 4:7–8).*

Gift-based ministry has been referred to by other names such as team ministry, networking and lay mobilization. Whatever you call it, gift-based ministry is a continuous ministry of the church that expects all members of the body to actively participate in the lifelong ministry task of service based on their spiritual gifts being used most effectively and pleasurably.

Establishing a gift-based ministry will create a beneficial transformation of pew sitters into active participants in kingdom building. Active congregational participation is a sign of a healthy church, and good health is necessary for growth. Church growth guru, C. Peter Wagner, lists "a well-mobilized laity which has discovered, has developed, and is using all the spiritual gifts for growth," as one of the vital signs of a healthy church.[5]

Discussion Questions

1. What process does your church use to nominate and select leaders? How has this process affected your church?

2. How can voting on people damage relationships and hinder church growth?

3. What is the difference between a democracy and a theocracy?

4. Why is it necessary for the pastor to have authority in the selection of leaders?

5. How much authority does the pastor of your church have in the selection of leaders? How has the pastor's degree of authority helped or hindered the selection of leaders in your church?

6. What are spiritual gifts? What is the difference between spiritual gifts and talents?

7. What is a gift-based ministry?

8. How could a gift-based ministry help your church grow?

CHANGE 4

Change from Teacher-Oriented to Growth and Purpose-Oriented Bible Study

Empirical observation over the years reveals that the primary aim of Bible study in many churches is the dissemination of information. In this teacher-oriented Bible study, both the teacher and the learner primarily consider the purpose of Bible study is to learn. Certainly learning God's Word is necessary and desirable. However, Bible study groups are also excellent vehicles for numerical church growth.

The key is to be organized for growth rather than just coming to learn. For example, by simply placing an empty chair in the midst of a small group Bible study and directing the group to invite someone to Bible study to occupy the empty chair will increase the number of attendees. Bible study

> **The key is to be organized for growth rather than just coming to learn.**

classes can be led to duplicate themselves through these kinds of organized challenges. Bible studies can be growth-oriented and purpose-driven.

A non-traditional Sunday School model called Fulfillment Hour exemplifies growth-oriented Bible study. Fulfillment Hour uses small groups to carry out God's biblically mandated purposes of the church during a specific block of time normally assigned to the Sunday School. Although the Fulfillment Hour model was designed to transform traditional Sunday Schools, the concept and the principles of the model can be used during any time period to transform Bible study from teacher-oriented to growth-oriented. Dr. James T. Draper, President of Lifeway Christian Resources, says this about the book, *Fulfillment Hour,* by Joan W. Johnson and Jackie S. Henderson:

> *Fulfillment Hour* is about how a church can fulfill all of the purposes and mission of the church through a systematic balanced and creative approach...It is a careful presentation of how it is done and how the same principles can be applied to any church anywhere.[6]

> **Changing from a teaching-oriented Bible study to one that is growth-oriented may be the most user-friendly change any church can make.**

The book fully describes the model and provides the theological basis and practical implementation procedures.

Churches that fail to organize their Bible study groups to grow are missing a golden opportunity for transformation and growth. Changing from a teaching-oriented Bible study to one that is growth-oriented may be the most user-friendly change any church can make because you don't have to start anything new. Most churches already have some form of Bible study. Also, due to the fact that the majority of the congregation probably does not attend Bible study, they have no vested interest in the old way. Churches who are sincerely interested in transformation should take advantage of this proven, user-friendly avenue of change.

Discussion Questions

1. What kind of Bible study does your church have? Is it teacher-oriented or growth and purpose-oriented?

2. How has your current form of Bible study helped or hindered church growth?

3. If your current Bible study is teacher-oriented, how can your church implement a growth and purpose-oriented Bible study?

4. If your church currently has a growth and purpose-oriented Bible study, how can you enhance it to help grow your church?

5. Why is changing to a growth and purpose-oriented Bible study the most user-friendly change a church can make?

CHANGE 5

Change to Embrace the Creative Arts

The questions here are: How many ways can you present the gospel? Is it sinful to present the gospel in any other manner than preaching, teaching and door-to-door evangelism? The mindset of the non-transforming church is that the gospel should be presented in a limited number of traditional ways. However, the spiritual gift of creative communication, which includes dance, drama, quilting and other artistic expression can be godly and effective ways of sharing the Good News. The message should not and cannot change, but creative methods of presenting the message are needed and welcomed in today's culture and society.

> The message should not and cannot change, but creative methods of presenting the message are needed and welcomed in today's culture and society.

As stated, the gospel cannot be changed. The message is: God robed Himself in flesh; stepped down through forty-two generations to be conceived by the Holy Ghost and born of a virgin; grew up in wisdom and stature, and in favor with God and man; ministered and healed; died on a cross; was buried in a borrowed tomb; rose on the third day; ascended on the fortieth day; revealed Himself in the person of the Holy Spirit on the fiftieth day, and now lives in us; and will one day come again as a king to judge the world.

This gospel should not be diluted or romanticized. The cross was rugged, not smooth or gold plated.

Jesus died a criminal, substitutionary death to save us from the penalty of sin. That is the gospel—the Good News. In how many creative ways can it be presented?

Don't misunderstand. The use of the creative arts is not intended to replace preaching or the preacher. The Bible says in Romans 10:14–16:

> *How then shall they call on him in whom they have not believed? and how shall they believe in him of whom they have not heard? and how shall they hear without a preacher? And how shall they preach, except they be sent? as it is written, How beautiful are the feet of them that preach the gospel of peace, and bring glad tidings of good things! But they have not all obeyed the gospel.*

This Scripture does not limit the presenting and sharing of the gospel to preachers only. The text says, *"But they have not all obeyed the gospel."* The presentation of the gospel through the creative arts may allow those who have not yet obeyed to obey. Presenting the gospel through the creative arts is not a replacement method, but simply another, and in some environments, a more user-friendly method, of sharing the Good News.

The power and effectiveness of the creative arts in presenting the gospel is that it paints a visible picture, which is often better than a thousand words. Every time I see an enactment of Jesus' crucifixion, burial and resurrection, I rededicate myself to the Lord. Mel Gibson's movie, *The Passion of the Christ*, with its realistic scenes of Christ's suffering, led thousands to accept Jesus as Savior. Many people who would not go to church went to the movie. Likewise, I believe more people would go to church if the gospel were presented in other methods.

Another advantage of using the creative arts to present the gospel is that it allows those with creative spiritual gifts to use what God has given them. To deny the use of the creative arts in ministry is to deny God a gift He has given to the church.

The difficulty with this change is not only the necessity of changed thinking and attitudes, but also money. Embracing the creative arts as ministry requires budget dollars. Also, most traditional church facilities are not built to accommodate the creative arts. Therefore, the feasibility and cost of renovation must be considered.

> The power and effectiveness of the creative arts in presenting the gospel is that it paints a visible picture, which is often better than a thousand words.

New church facilities should be built with the creative arts in mind. The church seeking transformation for the glory of God should not let anything deter them from embracing the creative arts. Our sole purpose is to reach people for Christ. We should use all that God has given us to do so. Without question, embracing creative arts will help the church reach more people for Jesus.

Discussion Questions

1. Is it sinful to present the gospel in a manner other than preaching and witnessing?

2. What is the spiritual gift of creative communication? In what forms may it be manifested?

3. How can your church embrace the creative arts in ministry?

4. What would be required of your church to support the arts? How would it affect your budget? What changes would need to be made to your facilities?

5. How would embracing the creative arts affect your church's growth?

6. In addition to church growth, what blessings do you see your church reaping from embracing the creative arts in ministry?

CHANGE 6

Change to Embrace Technology

The church's cutting-edge ministry must use every technology available for the purpose of kingdom building. Unfortunately, many churches have lagged pitifully behind in the use of technology. Society has changed, but the non-transforming church refuses to change. Communication methods and modes have changed. Not many years ago we were listening to music on breakable 78 rpm records. Shortly afterward we listened to music recorded on 33 1/3 albums, and then we enjoyed the use of 45s. By the 1970s the 8-track tape players were in nearly every car sold. Then came the cassette, the mini-cassette, the CD and now the DVD. We are living in a visual DVD era and many churches are still spinning old 78s, if not indeed cranking up the old Victrola.

> We are living in a visual DVD era and many churches are still spinning old 78s, if not indeed cranking up the old Victrola.

Technological advances must be utilized. Some of these include:

- Distance learning
- On-line evangelism
- PowerPoint sermons and lectures
- Video conferencing
- Digital printing, recording and photography
- Computers with the latest software for membership and financial record keeping

The face of the transformed church has changed, sound waves are balanced and faces are no longer looking down in hymn books, but looking up at screens. It is a myth to think that the use of technology is only for mega churches. (Although one of the reasons mega churches become mega is because of the utilization of technology.) Technological advancements are available and should be used by small, medium and large ministries. Refusing to embrace technology in ministry is a desperate last effort to hold on to the old church that we love so much. The seven last words in the final breath of a dying church are, "We've never done it that way before."

> It is a myth to think that the use of technology is only for mega churches.

The Internet must be fully utilized, not only for research, but also for church websites that allow members to receive communication updates, pay their tithes and offerings and review their financial contributions. The decision to use technology should be a no-brainer—embrace technology and be transformed or become extinct.

Digital cell phones, video conferencing, fax machines, Palm Pilots, e-mail and voice mail have made the world smaller and the opportunity for global ministry greater. Pastors and church leaders can minister in the uttermost corners of the world and be heard and seen at home. Pastors can now have staff meetings where they are seen and heard from the comfort and convenience of their hotel rooms in a distant city.

Pastors and churches should be equipped with technology not only for convenience, but also to better prepare sermons and Bible studies. No longer does one have to know Greek and Hebrew to study the Bible. Bible software is now available that gives the pronunciation, meaning and syntax of a word. A library of thousands of books, commentaries, dictionaries, and other references can be stored on one small laptop computer. Technological advancement changes so rapidly that it is impossible for anyone to communicate what is available from day to day. A leading educational resource for advancing churches and ministries entitled, *Technologies for Worship Magazine*[7] is a good source.

Discussion Questions

1. Why do many people feel that the use of technology in ministry is reserved for mega churches?

2. What forms of technology would help your church grow? In what ways could you use them?

3. What would it take for your church to implement the technologies listed in your answer above?

4. How could your pastor, staff and church leaders benefit from technology?

CHANGE 7

Change to a Coaching Empowerment Leadership Style

The key factor in church growth is leadership style, not preaching style. Leadership competence is the greatest variable in church growth, not preaching competence. This is not meant to diminish the role of preaching. Able preaching is necessary. However, there is more of a positive correlation between leadership style and church growth than there is with outstanding preaching. Good preaching does not grow churches. Good leadership grows churches.

There are great pulpiteers who pastor churches where there is no evidence of growth. Pastors across the country who listen to mega church pastors preach on TV, who themselves have defined and measured good preaching in a universal way, inevitably ask the question: What is his secret, because he sure can't preach? Many mega church pastors have been accused by traditional pulpiteers of not being able to preach their way out of a paper bag. The secret is leadership.

> **Good preaching does not grow churches. Good leadership grows churches.**

Most preachers, during the early stages of their preaching, seek to develop a preaching style that is different from others. Now that I have accepted and acknowledged my call to preach, how shall I preach? What is my preaching style? Whom shall I sound like? Oftentimes young preachers even listen to audio and video presentations of known great pulpiteers in an attempt to develop their own style. Either consciously or subconsciously, all preachers go through a stage of developing their preaching styles.

The problem is that the same process does not take place relative to leadership styles. Most preachers lead as they were led without questioning the effectiveness of the style in which they were led. Pastors need to study leadership styles as much or more than they study preaching styles. Leadership classes are necessary and good, but the greatest success comes when the pastor has a mentoring relationship with a person who has a proven record in church growth.

> Pastors need to study leadership styles as much or more than they study of preaching styles.

Leadership styles have been categorized mainly into three distinct groups: autocratic, democratic and laissez faire.

The autocratic style tends to be authoritative and dogmatic. The democratic style facilitates the process and allows the majority to make the final decision. The laissez faire style is a more hands-off approach to leadership. Laissez faire should not be confused with an unconcerned, don't care style of leadership. Laissez faire simply lets people carry out their responsibilities in their own way.

A careful examination of each style clearly reveals advantages of each. For example, in the heat of a battle there is no time to vote democratically to decide what to do. A clear, authoritative, absolute order must be heard to either charge or retreat. However, the advantages of the dictatorial authoritative style are short-term and limited. Churches whose pastors are purely autocratic will have limited growth.

Utilization of all of the styles is needed for maximum church growth. This eclectic style is that of a coach whose approach changes depending upon the situation and circumstance. It is the style that Jesus used. Jesus always did what was right according to the situation and circumstances.

The most distinct variable in the coaching style is not just the leader's ability to delegate, but also the ability to empower. Empowering means that once you have delegated the responsibility, you give the person authority to carry it out. In other words, you not only delegate the responsibility, you also delegate the power to get the job done. Delegating authority is not relinquishing authority as some assume and fear. The key to the coaching empowering style of leadership is to effectively manage the boundaries. The coaching leadership style defines the task, sets boundaries, empowers the people, and then manages the boundaries.

> **The coaching leadership style defines the task, sets boundaries, empowers people and manages the boundaries.**

Another distinct variable in the coaching style is "leadership multiplication." Coaches tend to duplicate and multiply themselves. In other words, good leaders make leaders. Poor leaders make only followers. "Leaders are learners. Until a leader learns the eternal laws of change, he cannot produce it in others."[8] Notice that this change is not directed at changing the congregation, rather it is directed at changing the leader of the congregation. If the non-transformed leader cannot change, there is no hope for the congregation to change.

The pastor is the catalyst for church growth. If the pastor is not willing to change and grow, there is no hope for the church to change and grow. Wagner states the very first vital sign of a healthy church is "a pastor who is a possibility thinker and whose dynamic leadership has been used to catalyze the entire church into action for growth."[9] Pastors and church leaders who are sincerely interested in growing their churches into all God would have them be will examine their leadership styles and change to accommodate what God wants to do. "The inner circle is myself," says Maxwell, "Change does not begin with the congregation, but with the pastor."[10]

> If the pastor is not willing to change and grow, there is no hope for the church to change and grow.

Discussion Questions

1. What is a coaching empowerment leadership style?

2. Why is it necessary for a pastor to utilize multiple leadership styles?

3. What type of leadership style does the pastor of your church have? How has it affected church growth?

4. How well does the pastor of your church embrace change? How willing is he/she to change?

5. What specific steps can be taken to implement a coaching empowerment leadership style in your church?

CHANGE 8

Change from Being Maintenance-Driven to Ministry-Driven

Keeping the Main Things the Main Things

The non-transforming church is psychologically and spiritually locked in a maintenance mode. Its prevailing thought patterns base all decisions on what they possess now. In addition, most of the energy of the church is channeled toward maintaining the status quo. Non-transforming churches either serve themselves, the institution, or the denomination, but rarely people. Maintenance-driven, non-transforming churches generally feel that the church's primary responsibility is to take care of the existing members rather than win souls and reach new members. The non-transforming church always reveals herself during budget time and when making financial decisions. The financial decisions are to repair, decorate, upgrade or remodel with little or no consideration for ministry.

> Non-transforming churches either serve themselves, the institution, or the denomination, but rarely people.

On the flip side of the coin, a transforming church emphasizes the need for ministry and ministry projects. Ministry can be defined as reaching out to help the lost and those in need while fulfilling God's purposes. Believers cannot expect to grow spiritually unless they are doing the work of ministry. Ministries must be established to accommodate and employ the spiritual gifts and talents that have been deposited in the church for edification (growth). All believers are called and equipped for a ministry task; therefore, ministries must be the defining point of the planning and implementation process.

Like the maintenance-driven church, evidence of being a ministry-driven church is always revealed in financial decisions and during the budget planning process. Jesus said, *"For where your treasure is, there will your heart be also" (Matthew 6:21; Luke 12:34).* Ministry-driven churches will plan their spending (budget) based on ministry needs.

Rather than one person or a small budget committee determining the budget needs, ministry leaders should be asked to make budget requests based on prayer and discernment of God's will. To be ministry-driven is to be purpose-driven. The primary purpose of the budget is the work of ministry.

> You can maintain a facility with money, but it takes the work of ministry to maintain and grow the spiritual life of a believer.

Ministries should be established based on the needs of people, rather than implemented just for the sake of ministry. In other words, ministry should be needs-oriented as well as Christ-centered. As Towns says, "The successful church will be relational, needs-oriented, relevant and aimed at helping people."[11]

A caution: Regardless of the number of ministries started to serve the needs of people, churches must be careful to remain Christ centered and keep the main things the main things. That is, all ministries should embrace the five mandated purposes of the church—evangelism, fellowship, worship, discipleship, and ministry/missions.

Being ministry-driven is essential to the growth of any church. You can maintain a facility with money, but it takes the work of ministry to maintain and grow the spiritual life of a believer.

Discussion Questions

1. What is a maintenance-driven church?

2. What does it mean for a church to be ministry-driven?

3. How can you tell if a church is maintenance-driven or ministry-driven?

4. How can being ministry-driven transform a church?

5. What specific actions can be taken to transform your church into a ministry-driven church?

CHANGE 9

Change Embrace Missions as a Lifestyle

A lot has been said about developing a healthy lifestyle relative to fitness and nutrition. A healthy lifestyle is more than behaving in a particular manner for a period of time; rather, it is an engrained way of life.

Transformed churches are healthy churches because they have embraced missions as a lifestyle. Although related, missions should be distinguished from ministries. However, both should be people-oriented. Missions always meet the needs of people outside the church; whereas ministry could meet the needs of the people within the church as well as others. A church can minister to each other, but their missions should always reach people who are not members of the church.

> Churches, like people, are healthiest when they help others rather than continuously think about themselves.

A distraught middle-aged woman, full of turmoil, came in for counseling. After listening to her problems, the pastor recommended that she participate in the church's Saturday morning mission project of feeding the homeless. Not really understanding the pastor's recommendation, the woman, out of respect for the pastor, decided to give it a try. The next week, she returned, thanking the pastor for healing her. Without taking any credit for her miraculous transformation, the pastor simply reminded her of Jesus' words in Matthew 10:39,

"He that findeth his life shall lose it: and he that loseth his life for my sake shall find it."

We simply feel better when we help others. We were created that way. Churches, like people, are healthiest when they help others rather than continuously think about themselves. We best serve ourselves when we serve others. Therefore, the transforming church should put its members on a steady diet of missions that will eventually lead to a spiritually healthy way of life.

Discussion Questions

1. What does it mean for a church to embrace a missions lifestyle?

2. How does embracing a missions lifestyle make a church healthy?

3. Why are we healthiest when we help others?

4. What can your church do to embrace a missions lifestyle? Be specific.

CHANGE 10

Change the Worship Style to
Expressive and Participatory

Worship style is a key factor in church growth. Some still hold to the thought that style is more cultural than biblical. Granted, worship styles are definitely culturally biased. However, the two key change factors, expressive and participatory, are unquestionably biblical. Biblically speaking, in most cases, worship is a verb, not a noun. The command is for all of us (not just the choir) to worship Him.

There are many forms of expression in worship, and culture may influence the various forms, but make no mistake about it, worship must be expressive and participatory. Studies and surveys show that growing churches invoke the presence of God through participatory praise and worship. The studies further reveal that non-growing churches are locked into a non-participatory, non-expressive style of worship. Prioritizing expressive praise is one of the seven critical church growth principles I list in *Faithful Over a Few Things*.[12] Expressive participatory worship is naturally more praise-oriented. God inhabits the praise of His people. *"But thou art holy, O thou that inhabitest the praises of Israel" (Psalm 22:3)*. The Bible also teaches us that we were created to praise Him (Revelation 4:11). Towns writes, "Worship is intended

> Growing churches invoke the presence of God through participatory praise and worship.

to introduce God's kingdom power in the church and extend that power through the church."[13]

Music and singing are key factors in worship as already mentioned in Change #1. I suggest that in addition to changing from art music to heart music, the transforming church should change the traditional period of devotion led by church officers to a time of praise led by a carefully selected praise team. Church officers tend to limit themselves to a Scripture, prayer and a long, drawn-out song. It is most desirable to have visible church officers lead praise and worship, but the key to change is when those in influential positions change. Just because individuals are officers in the church does not mean they are gifted to lead praise and worship.

> Worship leaders are not there to lead worship, but rather to worship and invite others to join them.

There is a special anointing that is needed to lead worship. Worship leaders are not there to lead worship, but rather to worship and invite others to join them. As a result, when the congregation participates, they experience what the praise and worship leader is experiencing. Praise and worship should not preach and testify. Neither should praise and worship leaders beat up on people or fuss about people who are not worshipping. The worship leader's task is simply to worship and invite others to share the worship experience. If the leader is anointed for the task, the result will be miraculously transforming.

Worship style sets the stage for worship's purpose. Worship is not a place, but something we do for a reason. The main reason is to express our love to God for who He is, what He has done, what He is doing and what He is going to do. Churches that desire transformation must incorporate expressive participatory worship.

Discussion Questions

1. Is worship a verb or noun to you? What is the difference between the two?

2. Why must worship be expressive and participatory?

3. Is it necessary for everyone to participate in worship? What if a person is naturally quiet and non-expressive?

4. Why should devotion be led by anointed praise and worship leaders instead of church officers?

5. What is the job of the worship leader?

6. When leading the congregation in worship, what are some things worship leaders should NOT do?

7. How can your church have a more expressive, partici-
    patory worship style?

8. How would having more expressive, participatory
    worship service help your church grow?

CHANGE 11

Change Something for the Sake of Change

Change should be thought of as good rather than bad. One of the reasons people don't achieve their dreams is that they desire to change their results without changing their thinking.[14] Change is a necessity in the Christian faith. Conversion is a change that is essential to salvation. Jesus told Nicodemus, "You must be born again" (John 3:3). Paul tells us when writing to the Romans, to *"be not conformed to this world, but be ye transformed" (Romans 12:2)*. Change should be thought of as a virtue rather than a burden. Proverbs 23:7 says, *"For as he thinketh in his heart, so is he."*

> Change should be thought of as a virtue rather than a burden.

Why then are we so reluctant to change? It is because of the weakness of our flesh. The flesh never wants to change. The flesh resists change. The flesh is driven by survival, thereby supporting the need to maintain the status quo. Therefore, a spirit-filled church is more likely to have a positive attitude about change. Churches that want to change their attitude about change must recognize and seek the presence and power of the Holy Spirit.

Churches that are among the "chosen frozen" will not change. The chosen frozen will become extinct one day because not being filled with the Holy Spirit makes change impossible. Towns quotes Bill Hybels as saying, "If the church does not change, its future is bleak. But its future can be bright if it's willing to be Spirit-directed and not flesh-directed."[15]

The transformed church views change as a necessary constant. In other words, in the transformed church, the only constant is change. Things are always changing. The transformed church has learned to expect change; whereas the non-transforming church resists change and remains completely stunted.

The question is often asked: Should we change anything just for the sake of doing something new? The logical, intelligent answer is no. However, the spiritual answer is yes. Change is so important to the spiritual growth of believers that there is really no such thing as changing for the sake of change. The sake of change is a good reason to change when it grows us closer to God.

> The transformed church views change as a necessary constant.

For attitudes to change, change must be practiced. For example, a church that practices walking to the altar to bring their tithes and offerings could change by simply allowing the ushers to pass the offering plate. Whereas, churches that customarily pass the offering plate could begin walking to the front to give their contributions. Some churches would even resist these simple examples because they interpret the Scripture that says, *"Bring ye all the tithes"* in Malachi 3:10 to mean bring your tithes and offerings to the front; however, God simply meant for us to bring them to the church. There is no doctrinal support for how a church collects the financial contributions.

Another suggestion that should not raise any doctrinal or theological issue is to simply have the members intentionally change where they sit in church on a regular basis. This is a tremendous exercise in the practice of change. Their flesh will not want to change seats. Their flesh wants the security and comfort of sitting in the same seat every Sunday. By the power of the Holy Spirit, have your members overcome the strength of the flesh by simply changing seats. I must warn you that this will not be easy, but it will be beneficial because it will demonstrate the power of the flesh and the need for supernatural help to change.

> **Change begins in the mind and is fueled by the power of the Spirit.**

Change begins in the mind and is fueled by the power of the Spirit. God tells us we are to be transformed by the renewing of our minds (Romans 12:2). Changing attitudes about the value of change is absolutely essential in the process of spiritual and numerical church growth.

Discussion Questions

1. Why is change a necessity in the Christian faith?

2. Why should change be thought of as a virtue rather than a burden?

3. Why are we so reluctant to change?

4. What is meant by the "chosen frozen"?

5. How does a transformed church view change?

6. How does your church view change?

7. Why is it good to change something just for the sake of change?

8. What are some simple changes your church could implement just to practice change?

9. What is meant by "Change begins in the mind and is fueled by the power of the Spirit"?

CHANGE 12

Change to a Systematic Strategy to Grow in Giving

here is a direct correlation between individual spiritual growth and numerical church growth. The key to spiritual growth is to grow in giving. Jesus said, *"For where your treasure is, there will your heart be also" (Luke 12:34)*. Churches, therefore, need a systematic, planned strategy to grow in giving. The Apostle Paul reminds us that as we grow in other areas of spiritual discipline, we are to grow in giving also.

> *But just as you excel in everything—in faith, in speech, in knowledge, in complete earnestness and in your love for us—see that you also excel in this grace of giving (2 Cor. 8:7 NIV).*

God is saying that we are incomplete until we abound in the grace of giving. Faith cannot be separated from finances. Giving is a faith walk. As our faith increases, our giving will increase. The effective stewardship of money is about raising faith rather than raising money. The emphasis should be on giving to increase people's faith rather than the church's budget. When faith increases, monetary contributions will also increase. To grow in Christ is to grow in giving. The Greek word for Christian giving is translated "God's grace." If we love Jesus more, we will give more. When we give more, we become more like Him.

The problem with most churches, especially the non-transforming church, is that except for some sporadic teaching on tithing, believers are not systematically challenged to grow in their giving. A transforming church that is committed to change will adopt a proven, systematic plan to teach and challenge believers to continuous growth in their giving. For all practical purposes, any plan of giving is better than no plan. Churches, like people, do not plan to fail. They fail to plan. An example of a systematic strategy for giving is "God's Progressive Giving Plan," which is a proven, step-by-step method for any church to change and grow in giving. Details of the plan can be found in my book, *Faith Raising vs. Money Raising*.[16]

> Giving is critical to spiritual growth, and spiritual growth is critical to church growth.

Again, giving is critical to spiritual growth, and spiritual growth is critical to church growth. If a church fails to grow in its giving, it will lag pitifully behind what God desires for it. Without an intentional plan to grow the members' giving, there will be no growth in giving, and there will be no transformation to create church growth.

Discussion Questions

1. Why is there a direct correlation between spiritual growth and numerical growth in the church?

2. Why do churches need a systematic, planned strategy to grow in giving?

3. Does your church teach tithing? Are your members challenged to grow in their giving?

4. If your church does not have a planned strategy in place to grow in giving, what can you do to implement an intentional plan to grow your members' giving?

CHANGE 13

Change to a Social Conscience and the Gospel of Liberation

Transforming churches minister like Jesus ministered—to the whole person. Holistic ministry must
have a social conscience and embrace the gospel
of liberation. In many cases, non-transforming churches
have not even heard of the gospel of liberation. Jesus is
not only Savior and Protector, but He is also Liberator.
God the Father says of the coming Messiah:

> *The Spirit of the Lord God is upon me;
> because the Lord hath anointed me to
> preach good tidings unto the meek; he hath
> sent me to bind up the brokenhearted, to
> proclaim liberty to the captives, and the
> opening of the prison to them that are
> bound (Isaiah 61:1).*

Jesus quotes God the Father in the Gospel of Luke and
applies the description of the ministry to Himself.

> *The Spirit of the Lord is upon me, because
> he hath anointed me to preach the gospel
> to the poor; he hath sent me to heal the
> brokenhearted, to preach deliverance to
> the captives, and recovering of sight to the
> blind, to set at liberty them that are
> bruised (Luke 4:18).*

These Scriptures give the purpose of Jesus' Spirit-
anointed ministry. Non-transforming churches often
make the mistake of interpreting His ministry as spiritual
and not a call to minister to the physical needs of people.
However, Jesus makes it clear that His ministry involves
the total person, physically and spiritually.

The church with a social conscience will minister to the social needs of people, such as poverty, imprisonment, unemployment, affordable housing, etc. The transformed church with a social conscience will not only minister to the social needs of people, but will also take a visible position on social injustices such as racism, discrimination and bigotry.

It is important to note that the gospel of liberation should not be interpreted as liberal theology. On the contrary, the point is to take a stand. Like people, churches that stand for nothing will fall for anything. Churches must take a stand on moral issues.

> A transformed church with a social conscience will not only minister to the social needs of people, but will also take a visible position on social injustices such as racism, discrimination and bigotry.

The gospel of liberation is about setting people free, not condemning sin. A transformed church that has a social conscience should have an economic empowerment initiative. Economic empowerment is not social welfare. It involves teaching people skills so they can take care of themselves and improve their quality of life. Most transformed churches have separate 501(c)(3) economic development corporations to manage this ministry.

Seeking out and ministering to handicapped individuals (the blind, the deaf, and the mentally challenged) is another way to minister to society holistically. Many of these individuals do not have the skills needed to organize to protect their human rights. The church will be blessed by being an advocate for the disabled and handicapped.

Churches that fail to minister to people's physical and social needs suffer from a "holier than thou" syndrome and can arguably be labeled as selfish. Selfishness is sin, and sin stifles growth.

Discussion Questions

1. Jesus ministered to the whole person. What does it mean for a church to minister to the whole person? What does it look like?

2. What does it mean for a church to have a social conscience?

3. What is the gospel of liberation?

4. What can your church specifically do to develop a social conscience and embrace the gospel of liberation?

5. How would changing to a social conscience and the gospel of liberation benefit your church and community? How would it help your church grow?

CHANGE 14

Change from Being
Membership-Oriented to
Discipleship-Oriented

Members come to church. Disciples bring people to church. Transforming churches are about the business of making disciples rather than just adding members to the roll. Actually, the Great Commission that gives the church her marching orders commands us to make disciples.

> *Go ye therefore, and teach all nations, baptizing them in the name of the Father, and of the Son, and of the Holy Ghost: Teaching them to observe all things whatsoever I have commanded you: and, lo, I am with you alway, even unto the end of the world. Amen (Matthew 28:19–20).*

Discipleship drives evangelism and healthy church growth.

The Greek text should be interpreted, "As you are going, make disciples." Based on this simple, informed interpretation, the word *make* is the only command verb. Jesus' instruction is clear: "Make disciples." Make disciples, and they will go. When we do authentic discipleship, evangelism will follow.[17]

Evangelism produces kingdom growth and church growth. Often the non-transforming church attempts to do the work of evangelism without doing the work of discipleship. This is like putting the wagon before the horse, which is an impossible arrangement. The horse is designed to pull the wagon. Likewise, discipleship drives evangelism and healthy church growth. A disciple's first responsibility is to go.

Discipleship does not and cannot take place in congregational worship. Worship was never designed to disciple. Discipleship best occurs in small groups and one-on-one. Transforming churches initiate a small group discipleship ministry that is supervised and monitored. All church members are expected to participate in the ministry of discipleship. Remember, when churches grow spiritually they will grow numerically. Becoming a disciple means growing spiritually. When believers grow spiritually, the church will grow numerically. A disciple is one who is a disciplined follower of Christ. A disciple's main purpose is to duplicate himself, i.e., to make another disciple. Therefore, discipleship is directly related to church growth.

> Becoming a disciple is about growing spiritually. When believers grow spiritually, the church will grow numerically.

A disciple not only learns about God, but also learns to love and follow God. Non-transforming churches engage in Bible study for information. Transformed discipleship-oriented churches participate in Bible study for the purpose of transformation. A disciple is one who loves God and shows evidence of a changed life. Disciples don't oppose change in the church because they realize that their lives are a product of change. A church that is filled with disciples will fill the church.

Discussion Questions

1. What are the differences between a membership-oriented church and one that is discipleship-oriented?

2. How does being discipleship-oriented help a church to grow?

3. Is your church membership-oriented or discipleship-oriented?

4. If your church is membership-oriented, what can you do to become discipleship-oriented? Be specific.

5. If your church is discipleship-oriented, what can you do to help your members become more spiritually mature?

CHANGE **15**

Change to Embrace the Holy Spirit and Acknowledge Spiritual Warfare

Change is impossible without God's Spirit abiding within the church. Our flesh is simply too weak to change. Change never takes place at the level of flesh. Change must occur at the spiritual level. Change is a supernatural event. To be saved is to be changed. When God changed us, He did it by the supernatural power of the Holy Spirit.

Transforming churches not only believe in the Holy Spirit, they embrace the Holy Spirit. Churches that embrace the Holy Spirit seek the presence of God in all endeavors. Churches that embrace the Holy Spirit realize that the Spirit is the source of God's power. Jesus says:

> *Wherefore be ye not unwise, but understanding what the will of the Lord is. And be not drunk with wine, wherein in excess; but be filled with the Spirit (Ephesians 5:17–18).*

It is God's will that we be filled with the Holy Spirit. The above Scripture is not speaking of possessing a spiritual gift, but rather it reveals our Christian duty. Every Christian is to be filled with God's Spirit. It is not a one-time filling it is a continuous process. It is our Christian duty to seek the presence of God through the filling of the Holy Spirit as we go, as we work, as we serve and as we worship.

Non-transforming, static churches doctrinally believe in the Holy Spirit, but do not embrace Him.

> Change is a supernatural event.

Non-transforming, non-growing churches treat the Holy Spirit as a stepchild or second-class citizen in the Godhead. They sing "Holy, holy, holy...God in three persons," but they act as if the Holy Spirit is not equal to the Father and Son.

Churches that do not embrace the Holy Spirit, do not attempt God-sized supernatural tasks because they don't believe in the supernatural power of the Holy Spirit. Churches whose believers do not seek the presence of God through the power of the Holy Spirit do ministry in the flesh and never reach the potential of what God wants them to become. Churches that are not Spirit-filled lag pitifully behind the transformed churches that embrace the whole Godhead—the Father, the Son and the Holy Spirit. The Holy Spirit being under-employed or totally unemployed is a common characteristic of churches that refuse to change.

Not embracing the Holy Spirit is linked to another problem that stifles church growth. Churches that do not embrace the Holy Spirit often do not acknowledge the existence of Satan and the need for spiritual warfare. Those that underestimate the power of the Holy Spirit also underestimate the power of the prince of the world. Not acknowledging the existence and power of the enemy is automatic defeat. Jesus tells us Ephesians 6:12:

> *For we wrestle not against flesh and blood,*
> *but against principalities, against powers,*
> *against the rulers of the darkness of this*

*world, against spiritual wickedness in
high places.*

Spiritual victory leads to church growth. Spiritual defeat stifles church growth. To win the victory, you must know you are in a battle, and you must know the source of your power. Your power source must be greater than the power of the enemy. Believers are too weak to battle Satan in the flesh. Addiction cannot be overcome in the flesh. Deliverance cannot be accomplished in the flesh. And yes, change cannot be implemented in the flesh. Churches that want to change and grow must embrace the Holy Spirit, and defeat the enemy.

> **Spiritual victory leads to church growth. Spiritual defeat stifles church growth.**

Discussion Questions

1. Many churches believe in the Holy Spirit, but fail to embrace Him. Why?

2. What happens when a church does NOT embrace the Holy Spirit?

3. What happens when a church embraces the Holy Spirit?

4. Does your church embrace the Holy Spirit? If not, why?

5. What can your church do to embrace the Holy Spirit more?

6. What is spiritual warfare?

7. Why do many believers not understand or acknowledge spiritual warfare?

8. How can acknowledging spiritual warfare facilitate church growth?

9. Do the members of your church acknowledge spiritual warfare? If not, how can you help them grow in this area?

CHANGE **16**

Change to Intentionally Prioritize Relationships

The dynamic, transforming church is intentional in its efforts to build godly loving relationships between God, members, leaders and communities. Ken Hemphill identifies six kinds of relationships that must be cherished and prioritized in order for the church to flourish according to the will of God. There must be a right relationship between the:

1. Pastor and God
2. Church members and God
3. Pastor and the members, especially other church leaders
4. Members and the pastor
5. Members
6. Church and the world[18]

Remember, church growth is a direct outcome of a right relationship with God, and right relationships with God are manifested in right relationships among God's people. In the church growth process, the word *relationship* is second only to the word *gospel*.

The operative word here is intentional. Deliberate, planned efforts must be made to give importance to forming and nurturing relationships. Some suggestions for intentionally prioritizing relationships are:

- Eliminate voting on people within the church.
- Tithe the church budget to missions.
- Teach tithing as a matter of faith rather than a matter of money.

- Preach, teach and demand obedience to Matthew 18:15–17.
- Preach and teach prophetically.
- Be people-oriented.
- Be constantly conscious of the need for organized administration.
- Create opportunities for the general congregation to show their appreciation and love for the pastor and his family.
- Assure the assimilation of new members through the establishment of small group ministries.
- Emphasize the love and unity aspect of the Lord's Supper or Holy Communion.
- Celebrate the arrival of new members into the family of God.
- Stress family commitments and responsibilities.
- Become proactive in demolishing strongholds in areas that have historically fostered poor and broken relationships.
- Be a living example by modeling the process.

The rationale for these suggestions and details on how to implement them can be found in my book, *Faithful Over a Few Things: Seven Critical Church Growth Principles.*[19]

Change is impossible unless trust has been established between the church and the change agent. The reason non-transforming, static churches don't grow is because of a lack of trust. If there is no relationship between the members and God, change will not be accepted. Many pastors take their members refusal to change personally, but the truth of the matter is people will not change when they don't trust God. If members don't trust God, they certainly won't trust pastors to implement change.

Relationships build trust. Pastors should not initiate change unless they have established loving, caring relationships with the members. In general, it is said that pastors must visit the sick, marry and bury enough members for an extended period of time (at least seven years) before a trusting relationship will be established that would permit them to be effective change agents. "The pastor of a growing church is typically a strong authority figure and that authority has been earned

> **Change is impossible unless trust has been established between the church and the change agent.**

through loving relationships with people. Pastoral authority earned through a loving relationship with the family of God is thus an important ingredient for growth."[20]

In the introduction, I gave three cardinal rules. A fourth cardinal rule is: "Don't attempt change until trusting relationships have been established."

Discussion Questions

1. Why is it necessary for a church to prioritize relationships in order to grow?

2. Discuss how the six relationships listed on page 91 affect church growth. What happens when these relationships are unhealthy or non-existent? What happens when these relationships are in right order?

3. How does having or not having a right relationship with God affect the relationships among God's people?

4. Why must there be an intentional, deliberate plan to make relationships a priority? Why can the church not allow the development of relationships to follow a natural course?

5. What are some specific efforts that your church can take to give importance to forming and nurturing relationships?

6. Why is trust essential to implementing change in the church?

7. What can pastors do to develop trust between themselves and their congregation?

8. Does your church trust your pastor? Does your congregation trust the pastor to lead them in transforming the church?

CHANGE 17

Change from Secular Order and Authority to Divine Order and Spiritual Authority

One of the greatest problems that inhibits church growth is the lack of divine order and the misunderstanding, acceptance and submission to spiritual authority. This change deals more powerfully with one of the basic premises of church growth. The church should make every attempt to come under total compliance and submission to the authoritative Word of God, even in her daily operation. Divine order is the total submission of the people of God to the Word and will of God in every aspect of congregational life.

Non-transforming churches are out of divine order when they operate according to the traditions of man and secular organizational structure. A God-governed theocracy is the divine order of the church rather than man's majority-governed democracy. Even popular, contemporary

> Churches are out of divine order when they operate according to the traditions of man and secular organizational structure.

churches whose members claim to be walking in authority have not realized that in order to walk in authority, they must first walk under spiritual authority. The church is not a Burger King; you cannot have it your way, even if your way seems the right way. The Bible warns in Proverbs 16:25, *"There is a way that seemeth right unto a man, but the end thereof are the ways of death."* Colossians 2:8 tells us, *"Beware lest any man spoil you through philosophy and vain deceit, after the tradition of men, after the rudiments of the world, and not after Christ."*

One of the greatest hindrances Jesus had in His ministry was overcoming the traditional interpretations of the Old Testament law by the Jewish elders. Their traditions had developed to a point where they were equal with the Word of God. Jesus' teaching and preaching conflicted with the elders' traditions. On one occasion, some Pharisees and scribes from Jerusalem questioned Jesus about His disciples not keeping the Jewish traditions.

> *Why do thy disciples transgress the tradition of the elders? for they wash not their hands when they eat bread. But he answered and said unto them, 'Why do ye also transgress the commandment of God by your tradition?' (Matthew 15:2–3).*

Traditions, legacy, history and heritage have their value. However, to hold tradition equal to the Word of God is sin. Churches that refuse to change because of traditional worship are guilty of having sin in the house.[21] Non-transforming churches are locked into human traditions that stifle church growth. According to Dr. Geoffrey V. Guns, in his soon to be published manuscript entitled, *Setting the House in Order,* the dangers of human traditions are:

- Traditions can blind us to fresh outpourings of God's Spirit in the church.

- Traditions can cause us to close the door on new growth opportunities.
- Traditions can lead to closed minds, negativism and spiritual stagnation.
- Traditions can be passed along to the detriment of the next generation.
- Traditions can become more important than God's Word.
- Traditions can kill spiritual initiative and motivation.
- Traditions can lead to generational error in belief and practice.
- Traditions can promote strife and division within a congregation.[22]

Churches that desire to change and do God's will, according to His purpose and way, must be transformed to accept, respect and teach spiritual authority. As Robert W. Puzimo states, "Authority denotes the power that persons display in the areas of legal, political, social, moral or religious affairs."[23]

Exousia (pronounced ex-oo-see-ah) is the Greek word for "authority" in the New Testament. It denotes the right or permission that is conferred for the express purpose of carrying out delegated responsibilities. *Dunamis* (pronounced doo-na-mis) is the Greek word for "power" in the New Testament. It denotes the capacity or ability to act.[24] Notice, authority is the right to act and power is the ability to act. Spiritual authority is God's divine, sovereign choice in the establishment of order and discipline for all of creation. Notice, spiritual authority is established by God. It establishes an order or hierarchy of authorities within all creation. Spiritual authority exists for the purpose of providing biblical government and spiritual order to the church.

Spiritual authority begins with the authority of God and the Word of God, which is manifested in the authority of Jesus Christ. Spiritual authority includes believers' authority and congregational authority. Believers' authority is the right of every believer to exercise his or her God-given spiritual gifts in the name of Jesus Christ and to engage in the work of ministry of the body of Christ. The congregation (the church) has been given the authority to go into all the world and make disciples of all nations.

> Spiritual authority exists for the purpose of providing biblical government and spiritual order to the church.

And Jesus came and spake unto them, saying, All power is given unto me in heaven and in earth. Go ye therefore, and teach all nations, baptizing them in the name of the Father, and of the Son, and of the Holy Ghost (Matthew 28:18–19).

Spiritual authority has also been given to the senior pastor and/or overseer of a congregation. The abuse of the senior pastor's spiritual authority has done more to stifle the growth of God's kingdom than any other single factor. The word *authority* is second only to the word *change* when it comes to stifling church growth.

Notice, there is a difference in spiritual leadership and dictatorship. This change is not a recommendation that advocates following a dictator. For a deeper discussion on the difference between spiritual authority and dictatorship, read Dr. Geoffrey Guns' book entitled *Spiritual Leadership: A Guide to Developing Spiritual Leaders in the Church.*

Submission to authority is gradually becoming a lost characteristic in our society. Children do not want to submit to the authority of parents. Students do not want to submit to the authority of teachers. Employees do not want to submit to the authority of the employers. Believers do not want to submit to the Word of God. Is it any wonder why church leaders, elders, deacons, trustees and congregations don't want to submit to the authority of the senior pastor? This abuse of spiritual authority can be seen when the pastor's vision, proposals and decisions are rejected by the members or have to be validated by a majority vote. It is even more evident when decisions are made without the pastor's approval.

> **The abuse of the senior pastor's spiritual authority has done more to stifle the growth of God's kingdom than any other single factor.**

Church leaders often believe and act as if they must protect the church from the pastor. The pastor is the undershepherd, not the underdog. The deacons are servant leaders, not watchdogs with the responsibility of keeping the pastor in order. Churches and church leaders who behave in such a manner are clearly out of divine order, and have no respect for spiritual authority. The authority of pastoral leadership is a legitimate, biblical right and responsibility bestowed by Jesus Christ, who is the Head of the church and who calls pastors into the pastoral ministry through the power of the Holy Spirit.

> **Pastoral authority should not have to be earned. It should be granted.**

Historically, pastoral authority is only established through the pastor-built relationship with the members and longevity. This takes time, and in most cases never really comes to fruition. Pastoral authority should not have to be earned. It should be granted. Churches that refuse to accept spiritual authority will remain out of divine order and will never grow to God's potential for them.

Discussion Questions

1. If the church belongs to God, how is it possible that some churches are not under total compliance and submission to the Word of God?

2. What is evidence of a church operating in secular order? In divine order?

3. If a church is out of divine order, how does it change to divine order and spiritual authority?

4. What is the difference in authority and power?

5. What is spiritual authority? How does it apply to the church?

6. How can use of the pastor's spiritual authority help or hinder church growth?

7. Has pastoral authority been granted to the pastor of your church? If so, how is it being used? If not, why, and what will you do to submit to God's Word?

CHANGE 18

Change from Casual Isolated Planning to Strategic Team Planning

Like people, non-transforming, static churches don't plan to fail; they fail to plan. Churches that refuse to change typically create their budgets in isolation, led by one or a handful of leaders. The budget is generally driven by the amount of contributions that were collected in the previous year and the need to maintain. To plan a budget without factoring in what you expect God to do in and through the church in the coming year is violating the commandment that tells us to walk by faith and not by sight.

According to William M. Easom, transformed, dynamic churches engage in strategic planning led by a general (the senior pastor) and accompanied by an army (the ministry team).

> The Greek word for strategy, *strategia,* refers to the plan of a general who has set up camp on a hill overlooking the battlefield. The idea is that the general has a vantage point from which to see the big picture. As the battle is waged, the general moves the soldiers and equipment in order to win the battle; but if necessary, he is willing to sacrifice some aspects of the battle to win the war. The Church of Jesus Christ is engaged in a battle for the souls of humankind. Every church needs the kind of leadership that can see the big picture, consider

> **Transformed, dynamic churches engage in strategic planning led by a general (the senior pastor) and accompanied by an army (the ministry team).**

the options, and make the strategic decisions that win the war.[25]

Strategic team planning helps the church discern the
will of God relative to its uniqueness. Strategic planning
helps churches lead, build teams and develop teamwork.
Also, strategic team planning helps the church and its
leaders identify the right things to be done and the right
way to do them. Strategic planning is hard work and spiritually challenging. It should not be initiated until the
church is prayed up and, as Nehemiah says, have a mind
to work (Nehemiah 4:6).

Strategic planning should work within the boundaries
of the vision God has given the pastor for the church.
Likewise, strategic planning should build on the church's
foundational and administrative framework, including
the mission statement, core values, job descriptions,
business practices, etc. If there is no foundational framework, the strategic planning team should begin by
building one.

There are several basic components of strategic team
planning. The first step is diagnostic and defines reality.
In the corporate sector, this function is known as a
SWOT analysis (Strengths, Weaknesses, Opportunities
and Threats). Churches that are serious about and
committed to change should consider conducting a Holy
Spirit SWOT analysis. This first diagnostic step is a difficult one, but absolutely essential. To bypass this step
could be likened to planning in the dark with blinders on.

The next step in the process is goal setting. Goals should not only be related to the overall church, but be made specific to each ministry or auxiliary. Goals should be SMART—specific, measurable, achievable, results-oriented and time-dated. Goals should be made public because a goal untold reflects a defeatist's attitude.

Another key component in the strategic planning process is accountability. It is difficult to hold each other accountable, but the value of doing so outweighs the struggle. When we submit to the accountability of others, we are saying we need help becoming all that God would have us to become. Often, when we think of accountability we only think of finances. A healthy transforming church must have good fiscal accountability, but it must also hold leaders accountable for their individual spiritual lives and the goals they have set for their ministries.

> A healthy transforming church must have good fiscal accountability, but it must also hold leaders accountable for their individual spiritual lives and the goals they have set for their ministries.

On the coattail of accountability is the component of assessment and evaluation. Strategic planning would be incomplete without assessing and evaluating the process and individual performances. This component answers the all-important questions: Did we do what we said we were going to do? How well did we do it?

The team approach to strategic planning could be the key that unlocks the door of change for many churches. It is certain that no church will remain the same after going through this process.

Discussion Questions

1. How does strategic planning help the church to grow?

2. How is strategic planning currently done in your church? Is it carried out by a select few, or is it done by the pastor and the ministry leadership team?

3. Why is it necessary to factor into the church's budget what you expect God to do?

4. Upon what foundational and administrative framework should your church's strategic plan be built?

5. Review the steps of the strategic planning process. Discuss how your church can implement this process to bring God's purpose for your church to fruition.

6. What is the importance of accountability in implementing your church's strategic plan. How will you hold each other accountable?

7. How will you assess the effectiveness of your plan?

CHANGE 19

Change Biased Perceptions of Church Growth

One of the most shocking discoveries in my twenty-five years as a pastor and student of church growth has been the realization that many members do not want the church to grow. The church certainly cannot grow if the members don't want it to grow and think that God does not want the church to grow. When I started on this journey, I made the mistake of thinking that everyone was like me and wanted the church to grow. I soon learned that was not the case. However, perceptions are real to the beholder. Therefore, in order for the church to grow, biased perceptions of church growth must be changed.

There are various reasons why church members don't want the church to grow. Many feel that if the church is large, it is automatically impersonal and they will get lost in the crowd, becoming only an envelope number. Others feel that the smaller the church, the more spiritual the church. Yet, others believe quantity reduces quality. In other words, more numbers lead to poor quality. Still others simply prefer to be a big fish in a little pond and fear becoming a little fish in a big pond.

All of these opinions are simply biased perceptions of church growth, and none of them are necessarily true. Small churches can be just as spiritually unfilled as large churches, and likewise, large churches can be just as spiritually filled as smaller churches. The size of the church has no bearing on spirituality, obedience or fulfilling God's purposes. Wagner writes, "Whether a church is large or small, it should be a growing church...One thing is for certain: a church must never stop growing. When it ceases to grow it will die."[26]

You often hear people say, "This church is too big." The question is: Too big for what? Too big to fulfill the mandated biblical purposes of the church? I think not. When filled with and submitted to the Holy Spirit, larger churches can more efficiently and effectively fulfill the biblical purposes of the church simply because they have more disciples to carry out the ministry of the church.

> **The number one reason why we should want the church to grow is because God wants His church to grow.**

The number one reason why we should want the church to grow is because God wants His church to grow. The great commandment of Matthew 28:19–20 is a commandment, not a divine suggestion. It is the last commandment Jesus gave to the church before His glorious ascension. It is the church's marching orders. This great commandment has no number limitation. Jesus did not say go and make disciples until you get a certain number of people or churches. He simply said, "Go." God desires that none of His little ones should perish (Matthew 18:14). Gary Hawkins puts it this way:

> "Growth is the most dynamic thing in life. Life is a gift of God to the farmer who grows crops. Life is a gift of God to parents who raise a baby, and life is a

gift to a pastor who leads a church. Growth means life, energy, new horizons, new freedom and new attainments. Growth means the fulfillment of expectations."[27]

Recorded in Luke 5:11 is what I call the Great Growth Commission. Jesus teaches us a lesson about fishing in deep water. He eventually called the disciples to be fishermen of men rather than fish. The church must realize that we are all called to be fishermen of men.

Some people even use biblical principles to rationalize their negative perceptions and criticism of church growth with such comments as "Church growth is not the main thing. Having a personal relationship with Jesus is the main thing" or "Church growth counts heads, but God counts hearts." Church growth critics often use the biblical narrative of Gideon, citing that Gideon had to lose some warriors before God gave him the victory to make their point. Again, there is no doubt in my mind that God wants His church to grow. I have often said that the church at her birth was the church at her best.

The following Scriptures from Acts (the history of the early church) provide evidence that God wants His church to grow.

"Then they that gladly received his word were baptized: and the same day there were added unto them about three thousand souls" (Acts 2:41).

"And they continued stedfastly in the apostles' doctrine and fellowship, and in breaking of bread, and in prayers" (Acts 2:42).

"Praising God, and having favour with all the people. And the Lord added to the church daily such as should be saved" (Acts 2:47).

"Howbeit many of them which heard the word believed; and the number of the men was about five thousand" (Acts 4:4).

"And the word of God increased; and the number of the disciples multiplied in Jerusalem greatly; and a great company of the priests were obedient to the faith" (Acts 6:7).

"But when they believed Philip preaching the things concerning the kingdom of God, and the name of Jesus Christ, they were baptized, both men and women" (Acts 8:12).

"Then had the churches rest throughout all Judaea and Galilee and Samaria, and were edified; and walking in the fear of the Lord, and in the comfort of the Holy Ghost, were multiplied" (Acts 9:31).

"And all that dwelt at Lydda and Saron saw him, and turned to the Lord" (Acts 9:35).

"And the hand of the Lord was with them: and a great number believed, and turned unto the Lord" (Acts 11:21).

"And a certain woman named Lydia, a seller of purple, of the city of Thyatira, which worshipped God, heard us: whose heart the Lord opened, that she attended unto the things which were spoken of Paul" (Acts 16:14).

"And when they heard it, they glorified the Lord, and said unto him, Thou seest, brother, how many thousands of Jews there are which believe; and they are all zealous of the law" (Acts 21:20).

Again, whether God wants His church to grow should not be a question or an issue. God wants His church to grow. Perceptions that are contrary to His will are sinful and should be changed.

> God wants His church to grow. Perceptions that are contrary to His will are sinful and should be changed.

In my book entitled *Breaking the Huddle,* I described the church as being in a huddle much like a football huddle. However, in football, the teams always break the huddle and run the play. The non-transforming church is in the huddle, and the play is to reach men and women for Jesus, yet the church refuses to break the huddle. Instead, the church moves the huddle from one location to another. If church growth is to take place, then churches and church members must change their biased perceptions about church growth and break the huddle.[28]

Discussion Questions

1. What are some common reasons church members do NOT want their church to grow?

2. Why should believers want their churches to grow? What does God say about church growth in His Word?

3 How does your church perceive church growth? Do your members want your church to grow?

4. Why are larger churches more efficient and effective in fulfilling the purposes of the church?

5. What are some specific actions your church can take to change its perception of church growth?

CHANGE **20**

Change to a Marketing Orientation
and Intentional Evangelism

What is marketing? Noted church marketing expert, George Barna, defines marketing as follows:

> Marketing is the performance of business activities that direct the flow of goods and services from a producer to the consumer, to satisfy the needs and desires of the consumer and the goals and objectives of the producer...Church marketing is the performance of both business and ministry activities that impact the church's target audience with the intention of ministering to and fulfilling their spiritual, social, emotional or physical needs, and thereby satisfying the ministry goal of the church.[29]

Marketing involves selling, and many churches feel it is disgraceful and distasteful to associate the church and the gospel with sales. However, in this case, we are selling Jesus and the gospel. I believe people who are sold on Jesus through marketing concepts are just as welcome in heaven as those who are persuaded to believe on Him through door-to-door witnessing or the invitation time that is extended to accept Him on Sunday morning. However, marketing is more than just a sophisticated word for sales. Marketing is a process or series of activities and not a single event. When church marketing crosses the line into a worldly or secular operation, it is the fault of the marketer, not the process.

Marketing involves promotion and distribution. In other words, you must get the word out and make sure your product is available. Marketing is the means, not the goal. The goal is to reach people and grow the church. Marketing is simply a means of doing so. The ultimate goal of marketing is the same as the goal of evangelism and missions—to save souls for Jesus Christ. Traditional evangelism activities may differ, but the goal is the same.

Marketing involves using mass media to ensure your target audience knows who you are, where you are and what you offer. A Christian church should not be the best kept secret in town. In his book *Marketing Your Church for Growth*, Gary Hawkins, Sr. says this about marketing:

> The name of the game is exposure. We must expose Christ to the world…The world is the audience. If we are to get our product in the homes of the unchurched, we must aggressively pursue to promote Christ to the world.[30]

The ultimate goal of marketing is the same as the goal of evangelism and missions—to save souls for Jesus Christ.

Marketing also involves imaging and advertising. Image is an intangible, but important part of a church growth strategy. According to Webster, an image can be defined as an impression by the general public, often one deliberately created or modified by publicity and advertising. All the visual images of the church (logos, signs, letterheads, advertisements and facilities) should come together to form one unified image. This is also called branding.

Advertising is a major part of marketing. However, advertising has its limits. According to *Can Advertising Help Your Church?:*

> Advertising will not change reality. Advertising will not convert people. Advertising will not cause personal growth. Advertising will not replace personal relationships. However, advertising will build morale. Advertising will create a climate for growth. Although studies still indicate that 70% of new members come from persons who have been personally told or invited to the church by a member, advertising creates the excitement and morale for personal invitations to happen. Advertising will attract visitors, and advertising will shape community attitudes.[31]

> **Because marketing principles, strategies and advertising are limited, they should be used in conjunction with intentional evangelism.**

In short, church marketing utilizes the "Four Ps" of effective marketing—product, place, promotion and price. Because marketing principles, strategies and advertising are limited, they should be used in conjunction with intentional evangelism. The key word is *intentional*, which means "purposeful." Effective evangelism does not just happen. There must be a purposeful endeavor with a directional focus. An atmosphere must be developed where there is a spiritual understanding of the purposeful direction. Also, evangelism must be the task of all believers in the local church. More often than not, the task of evangelism becomes the responsibility of the pastor or minister of evangelism, Sunday School outreach director, and a faithful few who feel they have the gift of evangelism. The task is not just for those who have a special calling; the call is for all believers. The prime reason for Jesus' coming was to seek and save the lost (Luke 19:10). If we are going to be faithful followers, we must intentionally make His agenda ours.

Evangelism is essential, and marketing concepts will enhance your evangelism efforts. Transforming, cutting-edge ministry will use all God has made available for the purpose of kingdom building and church growth. George Barna concludes:

> I believe that developing a marketing orien-
> tation is precisely what a church needs
> to do if we are to make a difference in the
> spiritual health of this nation for the
> remainder of this century.[32]

Discussion Questions

1. What does it mean for a church to be marketing-oriented?

2. How does being marketing-oriented differ from intentional evangelism?

3. How can advertising benefit your church?

4. What are the "Four Ps" of effective marketing? How can they be used in your church?

5. How can marketing and evangelism work together in growing your church?

6. Does your church have an intentional evangelism strategy? If not, what steps can you take to develop and implement one?

My Change Plan

Prayer Warriors	
Name	**Phone Number**

Goal	Target Date

Change	Target Date

Change	Target Date

Change	Target Date

Change	Target Date

Change	Target Date

Notes

1. C. Peter Wagner, *Your Church Can Grow.* (Ventura, CA: Regal Books, 1976), 14.

2. Elmer L. Towns, *Ten of Today's Most Innovative Churches.* (Ventura, CA: Regal Books, 1990), 31.

3. George O. McCalep, Jr., *Faithful Over a Few Things: Seven Critical Church Growth Principles.* (Lithonia, GA: Orman Press, 1996), 21.

4. George O. McCalep, Jr., *Stir Up the Gifts: Empowering Believers for Victorious Living and Ministry Tasks.* (Lithonia: Orman Press, 1996), 3.

5. Wagner, *Your Church Can Grow*, 187.

6. Jackie S. Henderson and Joan W. Johnson, *Fulfillment Hour.* (Lithonia, GA: Orman Press, 2002).

7. *Technologies for Worship Magazine*, 3891 Holborn Road, Queensville, ON, Canada L0G IRO; Web: www.tfwm.com; Email: info@tfwm.com; (905)473-9822; Fax: (905)473-9928.

8. Towns, *Ten of Today's Most Innovative Churches*, 25.

9. Wagner, *Your Church Can Grow*, 63.

10. Towns, *Ten of Today's Most Innovative Churches*, 36.

11. Ibid., 85.

12. McCalep, *Faithful Over a Few Things,* 58.

13. Towns, *Ten of Today's Most Innovative Churches*, 62.

14. John Maxwell, *Thinking for a Change.* (Warner Books, 2003), 8.

15. Towns, *Ten of Today's Most Innovative Churches*, 57.

16. George O. McCalep, Jr., *Faith Raising vs. Money Raising.* (Lithonia, GA: Orman Press, 2003), 11.

17. George O. McCalep, Jr., *Growing Up to the Head.* (Lithonia, GA: Orman Press), 12.

18. Ken Hemphill, *The Antioch Effect: Eight Characteristics of Highly Effective Churches.* (Nashville: Broadman & Holman Publishers, 1994), 72.

19. McCalep, *Faithful Over a Few Things*, 40–90.

20. Wagner, *Your Church Can Grow*, 65–68.

21. George O. McCalep, Jr., *Sin in the House: Ten Current Church Growth Problems.* (Lithonia, GA: Orman Press, 1999), 90.

22. Geoffrey V. Guns, *Setting the House in Order.* (Lithonia, GA: Orman Press, 2005), 11.

23. Robert W. Puzmino, *By What Authority Do We Teach? Sources for Empowering Christian Educators.* (Grand Rapids: Baker Books, 1994), 19.

24. Guns, *Setting the House in Order*, 36.

25. William M. Easom, *The Church Growth Handbook,* (Nashville: Abingdon Press, 1990), 109.

26. Wagner, *Your Church Can Grow*, 97, 103.

27. Gary Hawkins, Sr., *Marketing Your Church for Growth*. (Niles, IL: Mall Publishing Co., 2003), 47.

28. George O. McCalep, Jr., *Breaking the Huddle*. (Lithonia, GA: Orman Press, 1997), 71–81.

29. George Barna, *Market the Church*. (Colorado Springs: Navpress, 1988), 41.

30. Hawkins, *Marketing Your Church for Growth*, 3, 6.

31. "Can Advertising Help Your Church?" *The McIntosh Church Growth Network*, P.O. Box 892589, Temecula, CA 92589-2589. Vol 1, Issue 6.

32. Barna, *Market the Church*, 12.

THE AUTHOR'S COLLECTION

Committed to Doing Church God's Way

God has given me a burning passion for biblically-based kingdom building and spiritual growth. Through His Spirit, I have discerned and recorded in my books discipleship principles related to church growth, evangelism, personal spiritual development, praise and worship. I recommend the following titles to those who are serious about *doing church God's way*.

Church Growth and Kingdom Building

Faithful Over a Few Things: Seven Critical Church Growth Principles bridges the gap between theory and practice. It offers seven principles that, when faithfully implemented, will cause your church to grow. A study guide and resource kit are available. The resource kit contains a workbook, transparencies and a videotape.

Sin in the House: Ten Crucial Church Problems with Cleansing Solutions examines problems that hinder growth and offers proven solutions. This book addresses the question of why you and your church are not growing.

Fulfillment Hour: Fulfilling God's Purposes for the Church Through the Sunday School Hour by Jackie S. Henderson and Joan W. Johnson presents a nontraditional Sunday School model that fulfills all of the purposes and mission of the church through a systematic, balanced and creative approach within the context of an hour. *Fulfillment Hour* gives a detailed explanation of the concept, process and procedures of the model. The model can be applied by any denomination or church.

Evangelism

Breaking the Huddle contains twelve messages that deal with the central theme of fulfilling Jesus' purpose of seeking and saving the lost (Luke 19:10). Like a football team, the church must break the huddle; that is, leave the comfort of the sanctuary and obediently go out among the unsaved to share the Gospel.

Stewardship

Faith Raising vs. Money Raising is the most complete stewardship resource available today. It presents a biblically-based approach to doing stewardship God's way. The book describes a proven stewardship plan that can be implemented in any church and any denomination. It also provides advice on how to raise capital for building projects and includes a study guide and teaching aid.

Personal Spiritual Development

Growing Up to the Head: Ten Essentials to Becoming a Better Christian challenges the reader to mature spiritually by growing up to the fullness of Christ. The study is based on the book of Ephesians. The book uniquely relates personal spiritual growth to numerical congregational growth. The book is designed as a congregational study. A participant's guide and leader's guide are available for small group study.

Seven Weeks of Growing Up to the Head: Your Personal Discipleship Journey and Journal is an individual study of the ten essentials presented in the book, *Growing Up to the Head*. This study guide incudes daily lessons and journal pages for recording your reflections during your seven week journey to spiritual maturity.

Stir Up the Gifts: Empowering Believers for Victorious Living and Ministry Tasks is a complete, practical guide on spiritual gifts that is applicable for any denomination. The book is based on 2 Timothy 1:6 where Paul tells us to stir up the gift and bring the fire to a flame. Study of this book will fire you up and revolutionize the ministries in your church. A leader's guide and study guide are available.

How to Be Blessed: Finding Favor with God and Man is a biblical guide to being blessed according to God's Word. It is based on the truth that God promises to bless His obedient children. This book will protect you from finding out too late about all the blessings that were yours, but you never received.

When Black Men Stretch Their Hands to God is based on the prophecy: When black men stretch their hands to God in submission and adoration, there will be a revival in the land for all people that is unparalleled. I believe that God is calling black men to model for the world what it means to love God, themselves, their families and all mankind. Through their submission, God will use black men to bring reconciliation to all of His people.

However, reconciliation and revival must begin with knowing who we are and whose we are. This book affirms the biblical black heritage that has been ignored, misconstrued, misinterpreted and, in some cases, entirely removed. My goal is to eradicate ignorance, correct racist interpretations and affirm the existence of the rich heritage and presence of black people and people of color in the Bible.

Praise and Worship

Although the title is colorful, *Praising the Hell Out of Yourself* is a beneficial discipleship approach to praise and worship. It offers praise as an antidote for evil and provides the "how, why and when" of entering into His presence. A workbook, CD and T-shirt are available.

Inspiration

My wife's autobiography, *Tough Enough: Trials on Every Hand,* describes how God transformed a shy, reserved, country girl from Alabama into a bold, self-assured, yet humble helpmeet to her husband and spokesperson for the Lord. Her testimony of faith will encourage you.

Black History

A Good Black Samaritan teaches biblical black history—specifically how Jesus used people of color to teach the world what is good.

Resources by George O. McCalep, Jr., Ph.D.
Committed to Doing Church God's Way

ORDER FORM

QTY	ITEM	EACH	TOTAL
	Faithful Over a Few Things	$19.95	$
	Faithful Over a Few Things—Study Guide	9.95	
	Faithful Over a Few Things—Audio Version	14.95	
	Faithful Over a Few Things—Resource Kit	189.95	
	Breaking the Huddle	14.95	
	Breaking the Huddle—Sermonic Audiocassette	10.00	
	Growing Up to the Head	19.95	
	Growing Up to the Head—Leader's Guide	10.95	
	Growing Up to the Head—Participant's Guide	10.95	
	Seven Weeks of Growing Up to the Head	19.95	
	Stir Up the Gifts	24.95	
	Stir Up the Gifts—Leader's Guide	10.95	
	Stir Up the Gifts—Workbook & Study Guide	10.95	
	Stir Up the Gifts—Sermonic Audio Series	19.95	
	Praising the Hell Out of Yourself	19.95	
	Praising the Hell Out of Yourself—Workbook	14.95	
	Praising the Hell Out of Yourself—CD	14.95	
	Praising the Hell Out of Yourself—T-Shirt (L, XL, XXL, XXXL)	10.00	
	Sin in the House	19.95	
	How to Be Blessed	19.95	
	"Jabez's Prayer"—Sermonic Audio Series	19.95	
	A Good Black Samaritan	3.95	
	Messages of Victory for God's Church in the New Millennium—Sermonic Audio Series	19.95	
	Tough Enough: Trials on Every Hand by Sadie T. McCalep, Ph.D.	20.00	
	Fulfillment Hour by Jackie S. Henderson & Joan W. Johnson, compiled and edited by George O. McCalep, Jr., Ph.D.	24.95	
	Faith Raising vs. Money Raising	24.95	
	When Black Men Stretch Their Hands to God	24.95	
	Subtotal		

Order by phone, fax, mail or online

Orman Press   **www.ormanpress.com**
4200 Sandy Lake Drive
Lithonia, GA 30038
Phone: 770-808-0999
Fax: 770-808-1955

ITEM	AMOUNT
Subtotal	
Postage & Handling (Call for Shipping Charges)	
C.O.D. (Add $6 plus Postage & Handling)	
Total	

Name_____ Date_____
Address_____ Apt./Unit_____
City_____ State_____ Zip_____
Credit Card Type: ☐ VISA   ☐ MasterCard   ☐ AMEX
Credit Card #_____ Exp.____

Visit our website @ www.ormanpress.com
Your one-stop store for Christian resources!

Pastor and Sister McCalep are available to conduct
workshops and seminars on all of these resources.
Call 404-486-6740 for scheduling information.

Printed in the USA
CPSIA information can be obtained
at www.ICGtesting.com
LVHW091719140124
768932LV00061B/362